The Royal Forest of Dean
Gloucester and West of the Severn

The Royal Forest Of Dean

Gloucester and West of the Severn

Stephen Waters (signature)

Stephen Waters

Blaisdon Plumlications

First published in 2002
Blaisdon Plumlications
Spring Cottage · Blaisdon · Gloucestershire · GL17 0AL
e mail: bplumlications.aol.com

British Library Cataloguing in Publication Data

A Catalogue record for this book is available from the British Library.

ISBN 0-9543775-0-8

Printed by: Alpha Colour Printers · Waterwells Drive · Quedgeley · Gloucester · GL2 4AA

Acknowledgements

Any book that reaches publication only does so with the help, support and encouragement of many people and this is no exception. I must thank my wife Jean for the original idea, the photograph "Blaisdon Autumn Colours" and for input into photograph selection, not to mention checking my dyslexic spelling! Derek Foxton, who has published several books on Herefordshire, gave freely of his advice in the planning stages of the book. Miles and Richard at Alpha Print too have given invaluable help amd thanks to Rosemary for the plums.

I would also like to thank all the friendly, interesting and cheerful people I have met during my tours and walks around the Royal Forest of Dean.

Introduction

The Royal Forest of Dean has, until recent times, been overshadowed by the glamorous Cotswolds to the East. However, this beautiful area is becoming more widely appreciated and, as tourism becomes the major industry, replacing those of earlier times, the Foresters are sharing their secrets with visitors from far and near.

At its largest, the forest encompassed an area delineated by the Rivers Severn and Wye as far as Gloucester in the East and Ross on Wye and Newent to the North. Although never completely forested, the demands of industries such as shipbuilding, mining and charcoal production have been tempered by periods of planting and careful husbandry. The result is that the acres of bland conifers are balanced with beautiful areas of mixed deciduous woodland with the mighty oak its heart.

The diversity of the Forest is matched by that of the area as a whole. The majestic Severn with its mighty Bore flows along its Southern border whilst the smaller and more delicate River Wye sits on its West side. The Gateways to the area vary from the Cathedral City of Gloucester in the East to Chepstow and its mighty castle near the confluence of the two rivers. To the North are the county town of Monmouth, pretty Ross on Wye and the ancient market town of Newent. Within and along these boundaries is to be found an area of beauty, history and splendour…..

Gloucester

The majestic Cathedral of St Peter and the Holy and Indivisible Trinity still dominates the Gloucester skyline thanks to some fortuitous low-level building. Whether it is viewed from one of the surrounding hills, from nearby streets or as a backdrop to a cricket match, it cannot fail to impress. An Abbey until the Henry the Eighth's Act of Supremacy and the subsequent dissolution of the monasteries, it became the Cathedral of the new diocese of Gloucester.

The Norman building was extensively rebuilt in the fourteenth century in the perpendicular style. However, the great nave with its immense pillars was retained, though with a thirteenth century rib vault. Perhaps the jewel in this crown is the fan-vaulted cloisters whose delicate nature belies the large blocks of masonry used in their construction. The tower stands two hundred and twenty five feet high (sixty nine metres) giving splendid views over the town, towards May Hill and the Forest of Dean in the distance.

The spire of the redundant church of St Nicholas can also be seen close to the Cathedral at the lower end of Westgate Street. This is now used for exhibitions.

Opp: cathedral close and South Door

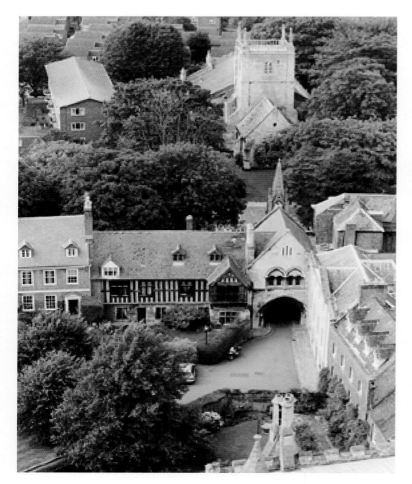

Another church close to the Cathedral is St Mary de Lode, seen here from the Cathedral tower. Originating from before the Norman Conquest, its name dates from the 16th century, being taken from a passage of the nearby Old Severn. During the Civil war, it was used as a prison holding Royalist troops.

Gloucester was, until the building of the Severn Bridge, the site of the last bridge crossing the Severn and had been an important town since Roman times. Its industrial history is varied, having been the centre for pin making and, later, match making at the famous Moreland's factory. The Gloster Aircraft Company produced many fine aircraft including the first gas-turbine jet-propelled aeroplane and the famous Gloster Meteor.

Opp: cathedral from the Docks

Granted the authority of a port by Queen Elizabeth the First, it was not until the completion of the Gloucester to Sharpness canal in 1827 that Gloucester became a busy inland port which large ships could now safely reach without being at the mercy of the tidal Severn. Alongside the river, the docks with their large warehouses reflect this, though tourism is now the major industry. The docks are home to pleasure craft with larger boats still putting in appearances from time to time. The surrounding buildings house the Waterways Museum, antique and craft shops together with restaurants and offices.

Opp: Docks from Cathedral Tower

Surfing the Bore at Over

The Severn Bore and Floods.

The Severn divides at Gloucester and there have been many bridges crossing both branches of the river and Alney Island between them. Since its opening in 1832, Telford's bridge has crossed to Over. The span measures 150 feet (46 metres) and has a rise of 35 feet (10.6 metres). Its attractive chamfered angles are designed to cut water resistance when the river is in flood. Now free from traffic, it is an excellent spot to view the floods that cover vast expanses of land and the Severn Bore.

Opp: Telford's bridge, Over

The Severn Bore is a tidal wave of water that passes up the river. It is created by a combination of factors that occur on the Severn, namely a large rise in tide (here up to 47 feet, 14.3 metres), a rising riverbed and a converging channel. Seen at its best during spring or high tides, it is affected by wind direction and river levels though the Bore can reach 6.5 feet (2 metres) in height. The river also continues to rise for some time after the Bore until the tide turns. It attracts large numbers of people along the banks of the Severn below Gloucester and some hardy souls also attempt to surf it!

Opp: Floods seen from Telford's bridge

Over and the Hereford to Gloucester Canal

Dwarfed by the modern roads, the small hamlet of Over can be overlooked but set among the new houses on the site of Over Hospital, is this beautifully restored canal basin. This is the work of the Hereford to Gloucester Canal Trust whose ultimate aim is to restore the canal between the two Cathedral Cities. The canal was completed in1845 only to be closed about 30 years later. Sections of it were later used for a railway line though this too is long closed. Other parts of the canal have also been restored including this lock and lock keepers cottage at Oxenhall, near Newent.

Westbury on Severn

Situated near the River Severn 6 miles southwest of Gloucester, Westbury on Severn has, as its main feature, the unique Dutch style water garden. Though both the original manor house and its successor have been demolished, the 18th century Tall Pavilion has survived and provides a wonderful overview of the garden with its canals. The garden fell into complete disrepair and was saved thanks, initially, to the efforts of some local people and, later, the National Trust. It became the Trust's first major garden restoration project. Using Kipp's 1712 illustration from Atkyns' *Ancient and Present State of Gloucestershire,* they have created one of Gloucestershire's most attractive gardens, though, sadly, the Yew hedges are under threat from flooding.

The parish church of St Peter, St Paul and St Mary is also unusual in having a detached tower. This 13th century watch tower has been surmounted by a later 160 feet (99 metre) spire. The frame is Forest oak and this has a covering of wooden shingles. Originally there was a small chapel attached to the tower but this was demolished in the 19th century. The origins of the main church building lie in the 14th century although many later alterations can be seen.

Garden Cliff

Near Westbury on Severn, where the Severn loops against rising ground, is *Garden Cliff,* the unusual name being a corruption of Garne, the medieval name for this part of the parish. The ascent is as high as 80 feet (24 metres) above the river and, as the cliff is eroding quickly, it gives an excellent view of its geology.

At the lower levels of the cliff are the red and tea green marls, the colours being due to the presence of minerals in the rocks. Formed from very fine lake mud, the rock is virtually structureless. When there was plenty of oxygen, the water and iron formed red ferric compounds. When oxygen was in short supply, green ferrous compounds were formed. Above these are the black Rhaetic rocks. These thin shales of ancient coastal muds are seen better here than anywhere else in the UK. Amongst these shales is the *Bone Bed,* a thin layer containing many fossils of fish, reptiles and coprolites (fossilised reptile poo!). It is also rich in pyrite crystals whose gleam gives them the name of "fools gold." At the foot of the cliffs can be found large slabs of Pullastra sandstone that bear the ripples of ancient seashores.

High Street and Clock Tower

Newnham

This attractive riverside town perhaps owes its origin to the presence of a ford and, later, a ferry to *Arlingham* on the opposite shore. As river trade increased, so too did its importance as a port and its wealth as a town. The High Street is lined with interesting buildings, many with Georgian frontages. Running down its length is The Chains, a grassy bank lined with lime trees and, in spring, covered with daffodils. At the lower end of the High Street is the Clock Tower, built in 1875. The church is, perhaps, the 6th on this site, earlier ones being lost to fire and the erosion of the cliff that continues today.

Over: Newnham from Broadoak

View from Popes Hill

Severn Views

Above Newnham, on the road to Littledean, is one of the most spectacular views of the River Severn with its great loop around Arlingham visible. The river can be seen meandering along its flood plan from Gloucester down to the Severn Bridges and its estuary beyond. Nearby hills such as Popes Hill near Flaxley also provide excellent views stretching as far as the Cotswold escarpment in the distance.

Over: View from Pleasant Style

Littledean

Continuing along the road away from the River Severn is Littledean, site of the Forest of Dean gaol. Built in 1791, this imposing building was considered a "state of the art" prison in its time! It has also been used as a police station, a magistrates' court and local record office prior to being sold to an insurance company in 1985.

Cinderford

The unromantic origin of this town's name is thought to come from the slag heaps left behind by early iron works. Its growth as a town occurred during later periods of iron working and coal mining, becoming the main settlement on the east side of the Forest. Mining rights are jealously guarded by a Miners Court and are the sole provenance of the Freeminers. A Freeminer has to be born in the Hundred of St. Briavels, the area at the heart of the Forest of Dean. He must also be over 21 and have worked in a mine in the Forest for a year and a day. The right of Freemining may have been awarded as a result of the miners helping in the battle against the Scots for Berwick on Tweed. A tribute to the Freeminers is to be found in the heart of Cinderford in the form of a statue shown on the next page. The artist is Antony Dufor who wonderfully depicts a miner working at the coalface.

Sitting in the once industrial valley that is overlooked by the town, is Cinderford Linear Park, also shown overleaf. This provides an attractive blend of wildlife conservation and industrial heritage. An easy stroll along the path of the Forest of Dean Railway from Ruspidge Halt towards Churchway runs for about 3.5 Km, passing ponds and wildlife along the way.

Flaxley and St. Anthony's Well

Lying northeast of Cinderford, in a narrow wooded valley is the village of Flaxley. Flaxley Abbey is thought to have been founded in1143 by Roger, Earl of Hereford to commemorate the death of his father whilst hunting in the valley. It was also a Royal hunting lodge with visits to the Abbey of various Kings being recorded. The Abbey became a private house in 1537 after the dissolution of the monasteries when Henry VIII gave the buildings and land to Sir William Kingston, Constable of the Tower of London. Most of the Abbey was demolished, however a late 12th century vaulted undercroft and other parts survive within the present building, which remains a private house.

The church started as a gateway chapel to the Abbey, becoming the parish church after the dissolution of the monasteries. Sir George Gilbert Scott designed the present building, which dates friom1856.

Further up what was once known as the Vale of Castiard, is a short path leading from Gunn's Mill to St Anthony's Well. The long held belief of this spring's healing powers can be seen from the large plunge bath, which is thought to have monastic origins. Water from the well is still used in local churches for christenings.

Over: St Anthony's well and Flaxley Abbey & church

Blaisdon in winter

Blaisdon

Thought by many to be the prettiest village in west Gloucestershire, 2002 has seen Blaisdon win the Bledisloe Cup for the best-kept small village for the fourth time. Famous in the past for its own plum, the Blaisdon Red, the once numerous orchards have all but disappeared, though many trees are scattered around in private gardens. John Dowding discovered the plum as a seedling in 1892. It was extensively grown and used in jam making on an industrial scale. A fire destroyed most of the village in 1679 though some buildings of that period survive alongside buildings of later times.

Blaisdon Church

Autumn Colour in Blaisdon

Blaisdon Hall

Situated at the north end of the village, the church of St. Michael and All Angels sits on a tump overlooking the Severn and beyond. The tower dates from the 14th century though the remainder was rebuilt in 1867.

Above the village, Blaisdon Hall has, perhaps, the best view of any house in Gloucestershire. Now a private house as it was when built in 1879, the intervening years have seen it being an Agricultural College, a school, a Silesian monastery and part of Hartbury College.

May Hill From the North

Mayhill

Named after the tradition of holding May Day celebrations on the hilltop, May Hill is the highest point in west Gloucestershire at 970 feet (295.6 metres). It is easily recognised from far and near by its topknot of conifers planted in 1887 to celebrate the golden jubilee of Queen Victoria. Earlier plantings mean that Mayhill has long been a beacon to the traveller. The site of a beacon at the time of the Spanish Armada, it is possible to see 12 counties and places such as the Malverns, Cotswolds, Sugar Loaf, Black Mountains, Long Mynd and the Wrekin

Mitcheldean

Nestling in a bowl surrounded by hills, Mitcheldean was a market town by the 14th century. It prospered as an industrial centre throughout the 17th and 18th centuries but declined during the following hundred and fifty years. The years after the second world war saw a resurgence with Rank Xerox operating a large factory centred on Wintle's brewery buildings, seen behind the church in the view taken from the surrounding hills. That era too is now passed, though the old buildings continue to be used by smaller and local businesses.

Although at first glance the centre of Mitcheldean has appeared to have lost most of its older buildings, closer inspection reveals much still remains, especially in the area around the church. There are three timber framed cottages in Mill End Street that date from the 16th century and provide an attractive row opposite the church. Old postcards show that two of the cottages had the timber rendered for many years and much smaller windows. The centre cottage was, for a time, the Jovial Collier public house.

The large parish church of St Michael has seating for 500. The porch and tower are 13th century; the spire was rebuilt in 1740. The church dominates this view of the town with the brewery buildings behind it and, further back, the modern factory buildings. In the distance, overlooking Mitcheldean, as it does most places within a wide radius, is May Hill.

Newent

Now an attractive town on the northern edge of the Forest, its appearance hides a busy history as an important market town and an industrial centre. Royal charters to hold markets were granted in the middle ages and the annual Onion Fair survived until early last century. It has now been revived. At one time Newent possessed iron works and its own coalfield. The Hereford and Gloucester canal passed nearby and was built to carry coal mined in the area.

Newent is still the largest town in this northwestern corner of Gloucestershire, in an area known as the Rylands after the local sheep or the Leadon Vale after the river flowing through it. Now, this agricultural area is also known for its daffodils, vineyards and cider.

In the town, there are some very attractive timber framed buildings including the 17th century Market House in the centre of the town. Later, many of the buildings were given Georgian brick frontages. There is also an attractive lake on the north side of the town and an arboretum on the western edge of the town. The lake started life as a series of fishponds for the local Priory and was later converted to an ornamental lake in the grounds of Newent Court. It is now well maintained and available for all to enjoy.

Opp: Newent Lake
Over: House and Market House

Ross on Wye

Standing above the River Wye, Ross looks as attractive from a distance as it is close up. This view of the town shows the River Wye in the foreground and the spire of St Mary's church rising skywards. Alongside the church is The Prospect, gardens that, true to their name, give fine views across Herefordshire to the Black Mountains. On the other side of the church is an interesting Gazebo Tower.

The centre of Ross is dominated by the Market Cross, built in 1650, replacing an earlier Moot Hall. A market is still held on Thursday and Saturday and the upper floor is used as an exhibition centre.

The Man of Ross, John Kyrle, was immortalised in poetry by Alexander Pope and Samuel Taylor Coleridge. He is remembered as a great benefactor to the town. He lived not at the hotel shown overleaf but in a timber framed building by the Market Cross. In front of the hotel is a sculpture of salmon leaping over a rocky weir. This very apt sculpture, given the proximity of the Wye and its reputation as a great salmon river, is by Walenty Pytel.

Nobler than Kings, or king-polluted Lords,
Here dwelt the Man of Ross! O Traveller, hear!
Departed merit claims a reverent tear.

      (Coleridge,1794)

Whose causeway parts the vale with shady rows?
Whose seats the weary traveller repose?
Who taught the heaven directed spire to rise?
  "The Man of Ross" each lisping babe replies. (Pope)

Kerne Bridge

The elegant bridge crosses the River Wye in the shadow of the ruins of Goodrich Castle, downstream of Ross on Wye. BD James built the bridge in 1828, the grey, green and red blocks of sandstone create a patchwork effect. Its five graduated semicircular arches together with its sweep across the river make it one of the most beautiful bridges on the Wye.

The bridge marks the start of the wooded gorge that takes the Wye through an area of outstanding natural beauty, passing Symonds Yat and Tintern before going on to Chepstow and the Severn beyond.

Symonds Yat

The combined East and West Symonds Yat villages and the Rock above must be one of the most visited places on the River Wye with their combination of beauty and visitor attractions. The latter include boat trips and, in the West village, attractions such as a maze. From 400 feet (123 metres) above the river, Symonds Yat Rock provides great views of the River Wye. The Wye passes almost completely around Huntsham Hill. This loop is nearly 5 miles long with the ends of the loop a short distance apart. This has fooled some visitors into thinking two rivers are passing close to each other! In walking to the Rock's viewing point, the visitor passes through earth banks that are the remnants of an Iron Age fort that is covered by the Mailscot woods. Peregrine falcons have a well-publicised nesting site on the cliffs and the Rock provides an excellent point to watch them stooping at speeds of up to 200 miles per hour.

It is possible to walk along the river valley from both of the Symonds Yat villages. Walking downstream, the Wye is found to be at its most seductive with overhanging trees and rippling weirs. Passing through the lower reaches of Mailscot Woods, Biblins Bridge is reached. This footbridge gives views up the river and down as far as the Seven Sisters rocks and allows the enthusiastic hiker to walk the banks of the Wye between the two Symonds Yat villages. Hand-pulled ferries are operated by the village pubs and will always provide the easy option for the return journey. They also allow a visit to the other side of the river without a long drive.

Over: view from Yat rock and East Village

Ruardean and Windril Point

Situated on the border of Herefordshire and Gloucestershire, Ruardean means, "Fortified hill." Ruardean Hill is 951 feet (290 metres) above sea level and once was the northern boundary of the Forest of Dean. The church of St John the Baptist dates from about 1100, its elegant spire, supported by flying buttresses, rising above the village and overlooking the Wye valley beyond. The surrounding green countryside hides a history of extensive mining for iron and coal as well as quarrying.

Along the road from Ruardean towards the Pludds is Windril Point. This provides extensive views over the Wye and Goodrich towards the Black Mountains, the Brecons, Sugar Loaf and Scirrid. Further round, it is also possible to see the Hay Buff, the Clee hills and the Malverns

Prior: Boat and Ferry at Symonds Yat

Cannop Ponds

These man made ponds have had nearly 200 years to shape the valley around them. They are fed by the Cannop Brook and were formed to provide power for the Park End ironworks. A large proportion of the surrounding woodland is broadleaved, principally oaks. Many of the oaks date from the early 19th century. Known as Napoleonic oaks, they were planted on the orders of Lord Nelson to ensure a future supply of oak for the navy. Thanks to the advent of iron and steel for shipbuilding, these magnificent trees are still here today for us to enjoy.

Sculpture Trail

A 3.5mile (6.6 Km) walk in the centre of the Forest of Dean has become a natural gallery to a number of art works that reflect and were inspired by the heritage and industrial past of the area, the artists being commissioned to give their interpretation. Each was designed for the surroundings it is now placed in, so both the sculpture and its natural environment can be enjoyed Since it opened in1986, sculptures have been added whilst some of the originals have been removed or allowed to slowly disintegrate back into the Land.

The works listed below, together with the names of their creators, are shown on the following pages:

Speech House

At the centre of the Royal Forest of Dean is the Speech House. It was built in1676 and though it is now a hotel, it also houses the oldest functioning court in the UK. The Vederers' Court is recorded from 1338. It exists to protect the Vert (bearing green leaves) and Venison of the Royal Forest. The four verderers are elected for life by the people of Gloucestershire and take their duties very seriously. It is interesting to note that all freeholders of the county of Gloucestershire, except those in the city itself, have the right to vote.

Across the road, opposite the Speech House, is a monument marking the centre point of the Forest. Alongside it is a suitably magnificent oak.

To the side of the building, again across the road, are the Royal Oaks. The right hand one was planted by Prince Albert in 1861. It was grown from an acorn taken from a tree planted by Queen Elizabeth the First in Pansanger Park. The other 2 trees were grown from acorns taken from Prince Albert's oak and were planted by the present Queen and the Duke of Edinburgh in 1957. Thus these mighty oaks connect the two great Elizabethan ages.

Over: Speech House and Royal Oaks

Soudley Ponds

Another series of man made ponds run down Soudley valley, though their original purpose was as fishponds rather than a source of energy for local mills. Built in the 1890's, today they are classified as a site of special scientific interest. The majority of the surrounding woodland in the nature reserve is broadleaf, including some "Napoleonic Oaks." These were planted on the orders of Lord Nelson. There are, however, signs that industry did encroach on this lovely valley, for charcoal hearths can be seen around the ponds indicating the great demand for charcoal by the local ironworks. Just across the road at the lower end of the ponds is the mill that now houses the Dean Heritage Centre.

Opp: Centre point of Forest   Woods at Soudley Ponds

Dean Heritage Centre

The home of the Dean Heritage Centre, Camp Hill is just across the road from the lower Soudley pond. The old mill house takes its name from the nearby ancient camp. Earlier buildings on the site include iron forges, though the present building housed a corn mill and dates from 1876. Later uses included making of leather insoles, a sawmill and a scrap yard. Now renovated, it houses a museum telling the story of the Forest and its people. The museum shows how the woodland and industry have coexisted through the ages and how the Forest continues to be managed today.

Blakeney

Blakeney grew at the confluence of two brooks, Soudley and Blackpool, providing the power for several mills. The oldest part of the village is around the church square, which is actually triangular in shape and has the main Chepstow to Gloucester road running through it. It still manages to retain its charm with attractive buildings, shown above, facing the church. The view opposite, taken from Blakeney Hill, shows the A48 curving round and down the hill, turning into the village in front of the church. Beyond, is the River Severn and the Cotswold escarpment.

Gatcombe and Purton

Gatcombe is a pretty riverside hamlet, whose potential as a safe anchorage and harbour was eliminated by the building of a railway embankment across its entrance. Drake's house, shown opposite, is named by tradition rather than fact. It sits next to the railway. It was, in fact, a public house known as the Sloop or Ship. Careful examination of the wall round it reveals this to be the old harbour wall as it curves round to merge with the embankment.

Sitting across from Drake's House are some fast decaying Stop Boats, a remnant of the net fishing on the Severn that has now died out. They present a picture of some charm mixed with a little sadness at their passing.

Purton was the site of the Severn Railway Bridge, until its demolition in the late 1960's. This followed the loss of two of its spans, brought down by colliding oil tankers. The only visible remains now are on the opposite side of the river where a pillar that used to support the swing bridge over the Gloucester and Sharpness canal survives

However, the railway between Gloucester and Chepstow runs alongside the Severn, giving passengers a view of the majestic sweep of the river. The railway line can be seen as it runs along the shoreline. Drake's House and Gatecombe can be seen in the distance and the picture also gives an impression of the size of the river.

Over: Fishing Boats and View from Purton

Lydney Park

Lydney

Lydney is a town with ancient origins; there was a Bronze Age settlement in the area. There are the remains of a Roman Temple built in an Iron Age hill fort that is now in the grounds of Lydney Park on the outskirts of the town. Lydney Park House was built in the late 19th century and is the home of Viscount Bledisloe.

Despite its antiquity, the town of today belongs to the last 200 years. The preservation undertaken by the Dean Forest Railway and, hopefully, of Lydney Docks is therefore all the more important. The steam preservation society is based at Norchard just north of Lydney. Trains are run through Lydney on the old Severn and Wye line. Trains cross the road in the centre of town, utilising one of the last manual gate crossings in the country.

Over Train at Lydney Town Station

Lydney Docks have a long history of being used for the shipping of iron, coal and timber from the Forest. For a short time the docks was also the site of a naval ship building yard. Today, a yachting club uses the harbour as a base. The only visitor of note is the Balmoral steamship on its twice-yearly trip up the Severn to Lydney and Sharpness. Those boarding have the opportunity to go down the Severn under both the Severn bridges and along the estuary to the north coast of Devon.

Over: Lydney harbour and The Balmoral

Clearwell

Clearwell like nearby St Briavels has a castle, though this is in fact a large castellated mansion in the Gothick style. After periods of neglect, it has been restored and provides a stately backdrop to local weddings and receptions. The village is larger than its older neighbour Newland. Clearwell gained its name from a nearby spring that is one of the main sources of the stream running through the valley. Nearby Clearwell Caves is an old iron ore mine that still produces ochre pigments for paints.

Prior: Upstream from Lydney

St Briavels

St Briavels gives its name to the Hundred of St Briavels where Freeminers' rights may be granted to those born within its boundaries. A Hundred was an administrative district that existed until the mid 19th century and was an area from which 100 men could be raised should an army be required. The original Mine Law Court was at St Briavels' Castle before moving to the Speech House in1676. With no maternity ward in the Forest, only those few being born at home will be eligible to be Freeminers in the future. Perhaps part of the maternity ward in Gloucester could be designated as an outlying part of the Hundred of St Briavels in order that the tradition may be maintained!

The castle at St Briavels is medieval in origin. It was once the administrative centre of the Forest. That, plus the 13th century iron industry, led to the village being considerably larger than it is today. However, the history of the castle is not notable and it was in a near ruinous state by the 1700's. The crown took the castle in the mid 19th century, undertaking repairs and, ultimately letting it to the YMCA. Once surrounded by a moat, a voluntary local group cares for the surviving ditch. Now, complete with wildlife pond, the area provides a pleasant surround to the castle.

Newland

The "Cathedral of the Forest," also known as All Saints' Church, Newland, sits in the centre of the village, surrounded by its churchyard. Houses bordering the churchyard date from the 17th and 18th centuries. Amongst the buildings are almshouses built by Newland born William Jones, a London Haberdasher who also founded The Haberdashers' School in Monmouth. The overriding impression of the vicinity is of a Cathedral close. This, together with the size of the church has led to its name, which is used with much fondness in the area.

Within this welcoming church are many memorials of interest. Perhaps the best known is the "miner's brass" depicting a Freeminer in working garb clutching his candle on a stick in his mouth.

Coleford

Although its origins may date to Roman times and it was a market town by 1661, Coleford grew with the Forest mining industry in the 18th and 19th centuries. The centre of the town still comprises mainly of buildings from these centuries. It is dominated by the tower of its former parish church, the remainder of the church having been demolished. The present parish church of St John the Evangelist is surely one of the most imposing churches in the Forest, towering over the town from its hillside position. Inside, its wide nave is dominated by the immense roof covering it.

Monmouth

This border town sits between the rivers Wye and Monnow and has thus been of major strategic importance since Roman times when it was the site of the first fort in Wales. The Norman castle is possibly the birthplace of King Henry the fifth. It dates from 1068 though there were later additions. The castle gardens contain only plants known to have been in cultivation prior to the death of Henry V in 1422. To its right is Great Castle House which now houses The Royal Monmouthshire Royal Engineers, the senior Reserve regiment in the Army.

The overview of the town taken from the Kymin shows the castle at the far edge of the town, in the centre. The Haberdashers' School for Boys is situated just over the bridge crossing the River Wye. The bridge dates from 1617 with additions to widen it in 1879. To the right is the spire of the parish church.

Monnow Bridge crosses the River Monnow at the lower end of the town shortly before it joins the Wye. It caries a 13th century gateway or fortification. This has been used for many purposes such as a gaol, guardhouse and dwelling.

Sitting on the Kymin is the Naval Temple, which was built as a memorial to the Navy in 1800. Its many plaques commemorate both well-known and almost forgotten naval battles and leaders.

Over: Naval memorial and Monnow bridge

Brockweir

This pretty village perhaps deserves a more attractive bridge, though, until 1906, there was only a ferry crossing. This did not impede the growth of Brockweir, as it was an important port as well as a shipbuilding centre until late in the 19th century.

Just downstream of the bridge is the Moravian Church. Built in 1832 and at one time attracting over 200 people to services, there was an agreement of union in 1963 between the Moravians and Baptists. The left side of the building is a residence.

Tintern

The beauty of Tintern and its Abbey had elicited admiration from generations of visitors, even before Wordsworth and Turner immortalised it. When Wordsworth first visited the Abbey ruins, the Duke of Beaufort who owned it had already cleared and grassed the interior. After a later visit, Wordsworth completed his " Lines written a few miles above Tintern Abbey." It was published in "Lyrical Ballads," a volume that also contained Coleridge's Ancient Mariner.

The Cistercian Abbey was founded in 1131 with the present building dating from the latter part of the 13th century, being consecrated in1301. Its life as an Abbey ended in 1536 with the dissolution. After that it quickly became a ruin though not an empty one. For two centuries iron wire was produced at Tintern within a thriving industrial complex.

However, with the age of "Romantic" tourism, the Wye valley in general and Tintern in particular became a popular place to visit. Today, set against the wooded Wye valley, the Abbey ruins remain one of the most beautiful spots along this or any other river.

How oft, in spirit, have I turned to thee

O Sylvian Wye! Thou wanderer through woods

How oft has my spirit turned to thee!

W. Wordsworth (1798)

Wynd Cliff

South of Tintern is the Wyndcliff, a steep limestone cliff that provides breathtaking views over the Wye. The river glistens below and Chepstow racecourse sits above the river bend. In the distance, the confluence of the Wye and Severn can be seen from the Eagles Nest lookout, as can the two Severn Bridges. Two paths lead to this point, one from the top of the cliff along a old drovers path, the other by climbing 365 steps up the front of the cliff!

Lancaut and Wintour's Leap

The river completes its turn beneath the Piercefield Cliffs and, as it rounds a hill that was the site of an ancient fort, the Wye passes below the white cliffs of Wintour's leap. Wintour's Leap was named after Sir John Wintour who is reputed to have escaped Parliamentarian forces by riding down the 220ft (61.5m) high cliff. Situated in an isolated spot beneath the cliffs is Lancaut church. A ruin for many years, this Norman church still has a serenity all of its own. The church font now resides in the Lady Chapel of Gloucester Cathedral.

Tidenham

As the Severn and Wye get near to joining, the land between becomes part of the same parish, that of Tidenham. Tidenham Church sits above the River Severn and is best viewed from the river as it is tucked into the hillside. Once seen from the river though, it is no surprise to learn that its tower has been a beacon for many generations of sailors. The train line runs close to the shore here also before turning in to Chepstow station.

Beachley slipway & Severn Bridge

Beachley

Sitting beneath the older of the two Severn bridges is Beachley. Until the opening of the bridge, the ferry from Beachley to Aust on the opposite bank was the only means of taking vehicles across the river downstream of Gloucester.

Beachley itself sits on a peninsular of land between the Rivers Severn and Wye marking the western most point of the Forest. Most of the peninsular is taken up by an army training school.

Chepstow

Alongside the Wye, the castle that sits so majestically overlooking the river and bridge has guarded this gateway to the Forest

of Dean since Norman times. Building started in 1067 with many additions in the next 200 years. During the civil war it was

held for the Royalist cause but taken by the Parliamentarians who used it as a prison. It finally fell out of use and into

disrepair at the end of the 17th century. This magnificent ruin remains an imposing sight standing right on the edge of the

cliffs overlooking the Wye. The elegant road bridge was opened in1816 and designed by John Rastrick.

Chepstow has a rich and prosperous history as a market centre, port and shipyards. Its medieval streets with many buildings dating back to the 18th century provide an attractive area around the castle. A large part of the 13th century town wall survives, as does the town gate sitting astride what was, until recently, the main road to the Severn crossing. At one time this was a tollgate. The upper room has had many uses including prison, museum, guardroom and living accommodation. The parish church of St Mary was originally a priory. After the dissolution, it suffered much damage but the tall Norman nave survives.

Severn Bridge and Chapel Rock

The older and more attractive of the bridges crossing the Severn near Chepstow also crosses the Wye just before the rivers join. It then passes over Beachley as a viaduct, before reaching over to Aust suspended from its two towers by almost invisible cables.

Opened on 8th September 1966, it replaced the ferry service overnight, providing Wales and the Forest of Dean with a rapid road link for the first time. Its walkway allows pedestrians to cross and enjoy the spectacular views over the two rivers from this most elegant of bridges.

Chapel Rock is an island only at high tide, this small rocky outcrop has had a chapel on it since the 13th century. Its dedication has been given various names, the most likely being that of St Twrog. In ruins by the early 18th century, little now remains and this is dominated by the navigation warning light situated on the island. It does however mark the extremity of our journey in this direction as the waters of the Severn and Wye mingle beyond the rock.

Over: Severn Bridge from Aust and Sunset over Chapel Rock

Bibliography

Over and Over Again	N. Bailey (2000)
The Cartulary of Flaxley Abbey	A. W. Crawley Bovey (1887)
Bridges on the River Wye	A. Crow (1995)
Geology Explained in the Severn Vale	W. Dreghorn (1967)
The Verderers and Forest Laws of Dean	C.Hart (1971)
Institute of Historical Research	Victoria History of Gloucestershire. Vols. 2, 5, 10.
A Glance Back at Mitcheldean	Paul Mason (2001)
The King's England: Gloucestershire	A. Mee (1966)
A Glance Back at Lydney Docks	N. Parkhouse (2001)
A new History of Gloucestershire	S Rudder (1779)
The Forest of Dean	B. Waters (1951)
The Buildings of England: Glos.	D. Verey (1976)

Index